A L

HISTORY

OF **GOLF**

KIM LENAGHAN   Illustrated by HELEN AVERLEY

APPLETREE PRESS

First published in 1996 by
Appletree Press
19-21 Alfred Street
Belfast BT2 8DL

Text and illustrations © Appletree Press, 1996

All rights reserved. No part of this publication may be
reproduced or transmitted in any form or by any
means, electronic or mechanical, photocopying,
recording or in any information retrieval system without prior permission in writing from the copyright
owner. Printed in the U.A.E.

A Little History of Golf

British Library Cataloguing-in-Publication Data.
A catalogue record for this book is available from the
British Library.

ISBN 0 86281 585 1

9 8 7 6 5 4 3 2

Contents

Definition of Golf

"To hit a very small ball into an even smaller hole,
with weapons singularly ill designed for the purpose".

Winston Churchill

Jeu de mail

The Origins of Golf

❦

The game of golf, or something very like it, has been played for centuries, but its actual origins are somewhat shrouded in mystery. Whilst Scotland is generally accepted as being the cradle of golf, a number of other European stick-and-ball games would lay claim to being its illustrious forebear.

The word golf probably derives from the German *kolb* meaning club, but some historians suggest that the sport actually dates back as far as Ancient Rome. **Paganica,** a game played in the halcyon days of the Roman Empire, employed a bent stick and a leather ball stuffed with feathers. In the first century BC the Romans began their invasion of Europe, bringing their popular pastime of paganica with them. The game became very popular with the locals, particularly in Holland, Belgium and France, where it formed the basis for many other games now considered to be the possible originators of golf.

Certainly a game quite similar to golf was played in Holland.

Called **kolf** or **kolven,** the name probably bears more similarity to golf than the actual game itself. Though sometimes played outside on ice, this was essentially an indoor game played on a smooth wooden floor in a rectangular area 60 x 25ft (18 x 7.5m), with a post about 5in (12cm) in diameter placed about 8-10ft (25 x 3m) from each end wall. Using clubs with straight shafts about 4ft (1.25m) long, the object was to knock a leather ball, the size of a cricket ball, from one end of the court to the other, hit the posts and bring it to rest as close to the wall as possible in the fewest number of strokes. In the case of a tie in the number of shots, the winner was the one whose ball was closest to the wall. Ultimately this game was more akin to billiards and croquet than golf. Based more on skill than power, kolven it is perhaps a more likely antecedent for hockey or ice hockey.

Another game that owes something to paganica was the French **jeu de mail**. Using a *mail*, a kind of wooden mallet, the players struck wooden balls over a designated course about half-a-mile long to a fixed spot or landmark. They counted the number of strokes taken to reach the target and the winner was whoever took least strokes to complete the course. Another similarity to golf was that each player could hit only their own ball during the game.

In Belgium, a later version of jeu de mail was the Flemish game of **chole**, which dates back to the mid-fourteenth century. This was played cross-country between predetermined

Kolven

starting and finishing points, with the object to reach the end of the course in a specified number of strokes. The implements for the game were clubs with long wooden handles and large iron heads which were used to strike an egg-shaped ball made from beechwood or leather.

One team would try to make the target within the declared number of shots, while their opponents tried to prevent them. First, the offensive side would play three strokes to move the ball toward the finish, then a member of the defensive team was allowed to hit the ball as far back as possible to where it had come from, or into any awkward obstacle that would impede the progress of their rivals. This backward stroke was called a *decholade*, and so the game continued, three stokes forward and one stroke back, to its conclusion.

Pell mell was another game, similar in concept to jeu de mail, which was introduced to England and Scotland from France in the sixteenth century. Mary, Queen of Scots, is recorded as having played pell mell and, later on, Charles I was a keen devotee. The English translation is "pall mall", and this was the name given to the original course laid out in London. The area still bears the name, though now it is a busy thoroughfare.

An earlier game played in England, during the reign of Edward III, was **cambuca.** Using a curved club, a ball made from feathers was struck towards a pin in the ground in an action a little like hockey. The game was so popular that it was actually banned from feast day activities in 1363 to encourage the able-bodied men of the population to practice their archery.

In England's Gloucester Cathedral a stained-glass window, dating back to the 1300s, features scenes from the Battle of Crécy in France. One image depicts a figure swinging a curved club. This is most often referred to as "the golfer" but the game being played was more likely to be cambuca.

But what of the Scots? It has been suggested that the game of kolf was introduced to Scotland from Holland through trading links between the two countries which were in existence since medieval times. This theory is supported by the fact that until well into the nineteenth century golf in Scotland was confined to the east coast, and surely if the game had originated in that country it would have enjoyed a larger geographic spread. Also, the earliest documented reference to golf in Holland dates from 1360 but in Scotland there is no mention until 1457. Given this evidence it would seem that the Dutch introduced the game of kolf to the Scots after all.

However, this theory overlooks one key aspect of golf. There is no record in any of the documentation on these supposed golfing forebears of that most basic element in golf;

the use of a hole in the ground. Whilst all these early stick-and-ball games have similarities to golf, all the targets used were above the ground. It was in Scotland that the hole made its first appearance in the game, surely proving that it is indeed the home of golf.

St Andrews

The Scottish Influence

❦

There is no doubt that the Scots were the true pioneers of the game. The Old Course at St Andrews lays claim to being the birthplace of the game and is undoubtedly the oldest links in the world in continuous use as a golf course, though there is an argument that it was in fact predated by Leith.

Wherever it was first played, golf was a significant Scottish pastime from the beginning of the fourteenth century, though the earliest recorded evidence of its popularity in Scotland dates back to 1457. In that year King James II banned the playing of "golfe and fut ball" by a Scottish Act of Parliament because he feared it was interfering with the practice of archery, the bow being the main weapon of warfare at the time.

However, the king's warnings fell on deaf ears and the Scots played on. So, after James IV acceded to the throne, a stiffer law was passed in 1491. This new law set a hefty fine and prison for anyone caught playing the game, an unpopular move not just with the masses but also with the nobility who were known to be keen devotees of the sport. Perhaps it was they who led the king to have something of a change of heart, because ultimately he became rather a fan of the sport he had tried to ban.

After James's conversion, the Scottish royals openly did an about face, and in the mid-sixteenth century golf became the object of royal patronage. James V was a keen exponent of the game, passing on his love of the sport to his ill-fated daughter, Mary, Queen of Scots. She learned to play at an early age and continued her hobby even while being educated in France. Apparently while there she christened the students who carried her clubs "cadets" and, given the French pronunciation of the word (cad-day), popular belief would have it that this is how the modern term "caddie" developed.

History tells us that Mary was a dedicated golfer who played at every opportunity. In 1567 she fell foul of the church for playing a round of golf just a few days after the murder of her husband Lord Darnley! It was also during Queen Mary's reign that St Andrews first came into existence; the citizens of the town were granted the right to use the links for golf by a charter in 1522.

Some years after her execution, Mary's son, James VI, ascended to the throne of England and Scotland. He shared the golfing passion of his ancestors and is credited with introducing the game to England. A seven-hole course was laid out on the sandy ground of Blackheath Common in 1608.

Such royal patronage was to continue down through the centuries, but golf proved less popular with the Scottish church. It seems that in some cases parishioners could face punishments, including excommunication, for indulging in their favourite pastime. Despite all this, the popularity of the game increased, and, by the seventeenth century the game was being played the length and breadth of the land.

By the middle of the eighteenth century it became apparent that there was a need for standarisation, and clubs and societies devoted exclusively to golf were developed along with a universal set of rules.

The earliest recorded club was the Gentlemen Golfers of Leith (later to become the Honourable Company of Edinburgh Golfers). Founded in 1744, this small group of enthusiasts

Scottish coastal course

played on the five holes of the Leith links until the 1820s when the company disbanded. It was re-formed in 1836 and moved to Musselburgh where it stayed until 1891. The club then moved to Muirfield where it constructed the great championship links, which is still the home of the club.

Most importantly, the Honourable Company laid down the game's original set of thirteen rules, the Articles and Laws in Playing at Golf. These were devised by the club's first captain, Duncan Forbes, and his fellow members to allow a structure for competitions.

On May 14th, 1754 some twenty-two gentlemen formed the Society of St Andrews Golfers. Then, in 1834, William IV conferred upon it the title of "Royal and Ancient" and became its patron. As the century wore on St Andrews became the accepted home of golf, as it still is today. The R&A was highly influential in the development of the game, decreeing that a 4½in (11.25cm) diameter for the hole was mandatory and stipulating that eighteen holes should constitute a match. In 1897 the R&A was requested to update the code of play developed in Leith, and it compiled the definitive set of rules recognisable to today's golfer.

Other notable clubs coming into existence at this time included Musselburgh, the Edinburgh Burgess Golfing Society, the Bruntsfield Links Golf Club and the Glasgow Club. But the majority of the famous clubs were inaugurated in the nineteenth century, particularly in the last three decades.

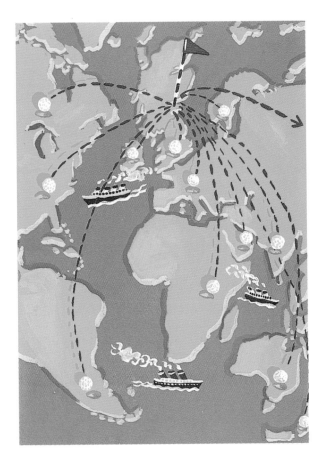

Golf Worldwide

❦

The first wave of expansion for golf was from Scotland into the rest of Britain. In 1864 there were around thirty golf clubs in Scotland and only three in England, but by the turn of the century this situation was completely reversed and of the 2,000 plus British clubs in existence, the majority were south of the border.

Of course, they did not all have their own courses and in most cases one course was shared by several clubs. Naturally it was the Scottish professionals who were imported south of the border to lay out courses and teach golf at the new clubs.

Just as the Scots brought golf to the rest of Britain, so too did they introduce the game rather further afield. Wherever pioneering expatriate Scots settled they brought their game with them. Among those overseas countries where they made their new home, none embraced the game of golf with quite the same enthusiasm as the United States.

It is known that the Scottish regiments who fought during

the American War of Independence, which began in 1775, played golf in their free time. But it was a century later before it really took hold under the guiding hand of John Reid, the man credited as being "the father of American golf".

John Reid and Robert Lockhart had left their homes in Dunfermline in Fife and settled on the east coast of the United States. Reid lived in Yonkers and managed an iron works, while Lockhart was a New York linen merchant who often had occasion to go back to Scotland on business trips. On one such trip, in 1887, he visited Old Tom Morris' shop at St Andrews and ordered six clubs and two dozen gutta percha balls on behalf of his friend John Reid.

When the clubs arrived, Reid got together a group of five friends - Harry Holbrook, Alexander P.W. Kinnan, Kingham H. Putman, Henry O. Tallmadge and John B. Upham - and took them to a cow pasture near his Yonkers home. There they laid out three short holes and built America's first ever golf course.

Reid and his friends were hooked, ordering more equipment from Scotland and searching out a new and better location. They eventually found a thirty-acre site at North Broadway and Shonnard Place, where they laid out a rough course of six holes with greens about 12ft (3.5m) in diameter. They played at every opportunity, particularly on Sundays, which led to their being sharply criticised by local clergy for desecrating the Sabbath, but just as their forebears in seventeenth century Scotland had, they ignored the warnings of hell

John Reid

fire and played on!

On November 14, 1888, Reid gave a dinner party for his golf-ing partners and during the course of the evening they formed the St Andrews Club of Yonkers. Reid became president of the new club, Upham secretary/treasurer, and Robert Lockhart, who had brought those first clubs from Scotland, was elected as a member.

In the spring of 1892 the club moved half-a-mile up the road to a 34-acre apple orchard. They laid out a new six-hole course measuring 300ft (92m) in length, and a large tree beside the home green became an unofficial club house providing shade and liquid refreshment. As a result the Yonkers golfers became known as the "Apple Tree Gang".

Whilst the members of the "Apple Tree Gang" undoubtedly laid the foundations for golfing in America, the game captured the public imagination and it wasn't long before they were joined by other clubs. In Middlesborough, Kentucky, a group of Englishmen constructed a nine-hole course and formed the Middlesboro Club in 1889, and by 1894 there were sev-

eral courses of six- and nine-holes. The floodgates were open, and by the turn of the century, just a few years later, there were in excess of 1,000 golf clubs operating in the United States.

The first eighteen-hole course was laid out in Chicago by Charles Blair MacDonald. He had become a devotee of the game while studying at St Andrews University in Scotland and on his return to the USA he persuaded his friends to build a nine-hole course in suburban Belmont in 1892, adding a further nine holes a year later. Seeing the merits of a longer course, the club then moved to a new eighteen-hole layout in a beautiful 200-acre setting in Wheaton, 25 miles from Chicago, a site that was to become one of America's great courses.

MacDonald was something of a purist when it came to the rules of the game, and was instrumental in laying down the laws of US golf. He was also a superb golfer and in 1895 became the first official US amateur champion.

Elsewhere on the American continent, Canada had also been influenced by those wandering, golfing Scots. The first club there was founded at Montreal in 1873, quite some time before John Reid's exploits. The Royal Quebec Club was formed in 1875, and competed in the country's first inter-club match against the Royal Montreal at Cove Fields in 1876. However, the spread of golf here was slower than its US neighbour, perhaps due to the smaller population and colder climate, though it has become a popular sport today.

Golf spread throughout the rest of the world with the nineteenth century expansion of the British Empire. The Royal Calcutta Club in India is one of the oldest clubs in existence and was founded in 1829 by Scottish golfing enthusiasts involved in trade with India. By the end of the century there were many other clubs right across the Far East and, in 1892, the Royal Calcutta Club inaugurated the Amateur Championship of the Far East.

The sport continued to grow and by the end of the Second World War, golf was universally acknowledged as the world's most popular sport.

The Necessary Equipment

❦

The game of golf would never have struggled out of its infancy, if the implements with which to play it had not been carefully developed to cope with the increasing demands of the sport and its exponents.

Of all the equipment necessary for playing golf, the ball has had the single greatest effect on the direction of the game, from club design to financial accessibility.

The earliest balls were made from wood, generally beech, but by the sixteenth century these had been replaced by the **feathery**. Despite being expensive to buy, easily damaged and difficult to make, these balls remained popular until the middle of the nineteenth century. They were handmade from leather and stuffed with boiled feathers, and even the most experienced ball-maker could only make four a day. This added greatly to the price, with balls costing up to five shillings each or a pound a dozen - much more than a week's wages for many enthusiastic golfers. Among the best renowned of the early makers of featheries were the Gourlay family of Leith and Musselburgh and Allan Robertson of St Andrews.

Apart from the obvious drawback of cost, there were other problems with the feathery; it was impossible to get a perfectly round ball, and the balls were soon knocked out of shape by wooden clubs or split in wet weather. Despite this, the balls were used exclusively until 1848 and the arrival of gutta percha.

Gutta percha was a black, rubber-like substance obtained by tapping certain tropical trees in India and the Far East. It was found to be soft and pliable when boiled in water and was easily pressed into the shape of a ball. It also kept its shape and hardened when cool, and if broken could be remoulded on

heating. The **guttie** was the ideal candidate to replace the feathery; it was considerably cheaper, longer lasting and could be made more quickly and in much larger quantities.

The balls could also be more easily standardised and makers

stamped the weight, between 26 and 31 pennyweights, along with their name on each ball. The best known balls of the time carried the brands of Old Tom Morris, Robert Forgan and the Auchterlonies. Gutties were also the first balls to feature the distinctive striations, later developed as dimples on the modern golf ball. The guttie was king of balls until the turn of the century when, like the feathery before it, it fell victim to progress and was made obsolete by Haskell's revolutionary rubber ball.

Coburn Haskell was a wealthy American amateur golfer who was certain that a livelier ball than the guttie could be produced. In collaboration with Bertram G. Work of the Goodrich Rubber Company of Akron, Ohio he developed a ball made from winding rubber thread under tension around a solid rubber core. The new rubber balls were placed on the market in 1899, but they were not an immediate hit. Whilst they travelled farther off the tee, they were lively and hard to control on the greens, earning them the nickname of "bounding billies".

However, the creation of an automatic winding machine coupled with the use of a pattern of bramble markings improved the flight of the balls. The final seal of approval came in 1901, when Walter J. Travis won the US Amateur Championship using a Haskell. All doubts about the new ball's liveliness on the greens were sensationally silenced and it went into mass production.

We know a lot more about aerodynamics today than our ancestors did a century ago, and as a result the surface patterns of the 1900s have been replaced by the distinctive dimples which accentuate the effects of lift and minimise the amount of drag on the ball. Modern technology has also made balls consistently cheaper and of a uniform size. In 1921 the United States Golf Association and the Royal and Ancient agreed that all balls should be 1.62in (4cm) in diameter, but a decade later the USGA increased the size to 1.68in (4.2cm). Finally, in 1987, this measurement was also accepted by the R&A and the American size is now the standard.

The quest for the perfect golf ball may have taken centuries, but the development of the perfect club is as old as the game itself. The earliest golf clubs, dating back to the fifteenth century, were fairly rudimentary, just a solid wooden shaft, a weighted head and a padded handle bound with animal hide. It was not until the beginning of the eighteenth century that metal headed clubs made an appearance.

The long-nosed, long-shafted playclub dominated golf in the eighteenth and nineteenth centuries, and by the mid-1800s clubs could be divided into four categories, drivers, spoons, irons and putters. There were two sorts of drivers - the **playclub driver** which had a flat face, no loft and was designed to hit a ball off a tee, and the **grassed driver**, slightly lofted to lift the ball from a hazard or downhill lie. There were four types of spoons - long, middle, short and baffing. The **baffy**, as it was known, was short and stiff with a laid-back face and was used for pitching to the green. The wooden **niblick** was short, well

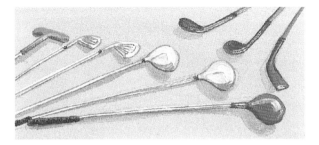

lofted and made with a small head so that it could cut through heavy grass. Wooden putters were used for centuries and were ideal on rougher greens but, as the playing surfaces improved, the smoother, iron blade became the popular choice.

The early irons were very heavy, rather fearsome looking and ideal for the big hitters. They were hand forged with a socket into which the finely tapered shaft was fitted and driven into the club head to give a tight fit. Initially irons were not widely used because of the delicate nature of the feather balls, but by the mid-nineteenth century and the advent of the gutta percha and rubber balls they came into their own.

The heads of the wooden clubs were made mostly from fruitwoods: hornbeam; thornwood; beech and persimmon, a wood imported from North America. The shafts were joined to the underside of the neck of the clubhead by a simple splice and held tightly using a tarred twine binding. These shafts, made

from ash, hazel and hickory, were slender and finely tapered to ensure the "spring" was in the right position. The grips were made of stuff strips covered with leather and nailed to the shaft.

The arrival of the guttie had a marked effect on club design, and they became shorter, broader and deeper with new clubs like the **bulger** being developed. This was a driver with a distinctive convex face and was designed to minimise a sliced or hooked stroke. Another new club was the **brassie**, which took its name from its brass sole and was designed to play off hard surfaces. Iron clubs also increased in popularity, primarily because they were cheaper to manufacture and, as has already been mentioned, could not harm the new style balls.

By the turn of the century a set of irons, each with a different degree of loft, comprised: the driving cleek; iron cleek; lofter; mashie; sand iron; niblick and putting cleek. Clubs with aluminium heads made their first appearance during this period, first as putters and then as a full range of clubs.

The most significant advance in the early part of the twentieth century was the introduction of the steel shaft. The first seamless, steel shafts were produced in Britain in 1912 and during the next two decades steel also became widely used in the United States. Nevertheless, it was only in 1929 that the R&A legalised the use of steel shafts, and only then because the Prince of Wales, later the abdicating Edward VIII, played with a set of steel shafted clubs at St Andrews and it seemed they had little choice but to accede to the wishes of their future king.

Mass-produced clubs followed and with them came matched sets with numbered rather than named clubs. Soon there were clubs for every possible situation and some golfers were carrying huge numbers of clubs on each round. To combat this and force the golfer to rely once more on his skill and not just his clubs, the United States Golfing Association imposed a fourteen club limit in 1938 and the Royal and Ancient took similar action a year later.

Recently, most manufacturers have geared production toward game improvement with peripherally-weighted irons and customised clubs which are now widely available. Steel is still the main constituent in making shafts for irons, but carbon fibre or graphite is becoming a more popular choice because of its light weight and high strength. It is also increasingly being used for clubheads.

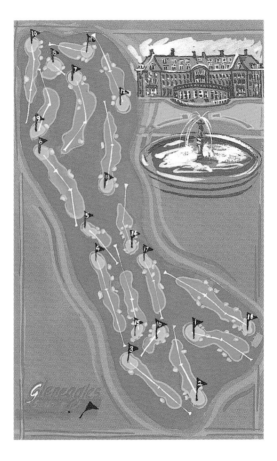

Gleneagles course

On Course

❦

The greatest course architect of all time is nature and those glorious early links, cut in great swathes of coast and dunes are among its finest achievements, particularly at the birthplace of golf on the east coast of Scotland. But nature couldn't keep pace with the passion for golf and some man-made intervention was required.

Early courses were laid out within one day. These were very simply designed and the links land was transformed into a golf course by cutting holes, marking greens with coloured stakes and excavating bunkers in accordance with the natural terrain.

Until golf course architecture became a profession at the end of the nineteenth century, man didn't necessarily do a particularly great job shaping the gifts nature gave him. Dr Alister Mackenzie, the great golf architect who collaborated in the creation of Augusta National in the United States, suggested in 1920:

"I believe the real reason St Andrews Old Course is infinitely superior to anything else is owing to the fact that it was constructed when no one knew anything about the subject at all, and since then it has been considered too sacred to be touched."

The desire to appear natural was as important one hundred years ago as it is now. Indeed, it was originally believed that only naturally well-endowed links courses were truly suitable for the playing of golf, but that was before the efforts of the last century's army of talented architects, led by Old Tom Morris. He was one of the greatest golf professionals of his day and the courses he laid out are legendary. His approach was simple, though he used a great deal of imagination trying to avoid the standard nine holes out and nine holes back, and this is particularly notable in the courses he designed at Muirfield in Scotland and Royal County Down in Northern Ireland.

That was all very well with such fine raw material, but many of the early parkland courses were appalling, and arch critic Alister Mackenzie again did a great job of summing up their faults:

"Golf, on a good links is, in all probability, the best game in the world, but on the late-Victorian type of inland course, where there is a complete lack of variety, flat fairways, flat unguarded greens, long grass, necessitating frequent searching for lost balls, and mathemati-

cally placed hazards consisting of the cop or pimple variety, it not only offends all the finest instincts of the artist and sportsman, but it is the most boring game in existence."

But all this changed with the realisation that the best turf for golf courses was the least suitable for farming. The sandy subsoil of the heathlands to the south and west of London was the perfect foundation for a golf course and it highlighted the way forward for the development of inland sites. This was most ably proven by pioneering golf professional Willie Park Jnr, son of the first Open champion and twice a winner himself, who laid out the first course at Sunningdale in the 1890s. His lead was followed by other golf professionals like Harry Colt, who laid out the New Course at Sunningdale, and five times Open winner, James Braid, who designed the courses at Gleneagles.

Jack Nicklaus

Across the Atlantic, in 1902, Charles Blair MacDonald, architect of the Chicago golf-course, began researching British golf courses which assisted him greatly in designing the renowned National Golf Course in the USA. His example inspired other architects like George Crump, A.W. Tillinghast and Hugh Wilson to create the courses at Pine Valley, Baltusrol and Merion. Donald Ross, a Scot, designed some legendary courses in the States, among them Pinehurst Number 2, and fellow countryman Alister Mackenzie partnered Bobby Jones in creating Augusta National. The strategic approach used for these courses revolutionised course design in the United States.

Following his somewhat controversial adaptation of the Oakland Hills course in Michigan for the 1951 US Open, Robert Trent Jones became the leading golf course architect in the United States, and during the 1960s and 70s his trademark lakes amid massive bunkers were stamped on courses right across the country.

In the late 1960s, Pete Dye teamed up with professional golfer Jack Nicklaus to develop the Harbour Town Golf Links in South Carolina and the two have gone on to become the best course designers in the late twentieth century. As in the early days, golf professionals are once again dominating the field of golf course design. Arnold Palmer, Seve Ballesteros, Bernhard Langer and Tony Jacklin, to name only a few, are putting their mark and their name on courses around the globe, and there certainly is a steady demand for more of the same.

Letting in the Ladies

❦

G iven their notable absence in the preceding chapters of this book, you will have gathered by now that women's golf has never attracted the same interest as men's, particularly on the professional circuit, although women have been playing the game for just as long.

We know that Mary, Queen of Scots and many of her fellow female nobility were ardent golfers, but from the sixteenth century on there seems to be only scant reference to women's role in the game. There is no logical explanation for this, except that as the game developed and became more strenuous it may not have seemed quite ladylike enough. Add to this some of the ridiculous and restrictive fashions worn by women in the last three centuries and the playing of most active sports, not just golf, must have been virtually impossible. To cap it all, along came the golf club which, until relatively recently, was generally an all-male preserve with women strictly forbidden.

Despite all this, a few well-heeled ladies did take up the

Glenna Collet

sport in the nineteenth century, but in a rather limited way. It was considered somewhat indelicate to raise a club above shoulder height, not that their full skirts and corsets would have allowed that in any case, and balls were merely struck along the ground, not unlike croquet.

Things were changing though and women began to form their own clubs and develop a more suitable attire. In 1893 the Ladies Golf Union was formed in Britain and blossomed under the direction of its secretary Issette Pearson, a keen golfer and runner-up to Lady Margaret Scott in the first British Ladies' Amateur Championship held that same year.

Times were changing on the other side of the Atlantic too, and members of New York's Shinnecock Hills Club were persuaded by their wives to build them their own nine-hole course. By 1894 a group of female golfers had founded their own club and created a seven-hole course in Morristown, New Jersey.

The first big name in women's golf in Britain was Cecil (short for Cecilia) Leitch. When she was just 17 she reached the semi-finals of the 1908 British Ladies' Amateur and went on to dominate the ladies' game, winning twelve titles in Britain, Canada and France. Her trademark swing - forceful and flat - was in direct contrast to that of Joyce Wethered (Lady Heathcoat-Amory) who was noted for her elegant, stylish swing, admired by male as well as female golfers. Wethered's record in competitive golf was outstanding: she scooped five consecutive English Ladies' Championships from 1920-1924. She retired in 1925 but made a comeback four years later to win the British Ladies' title for a fourth time, beating US Ladies' Champion Glenna Collet.

Just as Wethered dominated the game in Britain, so Collet did in the United States where she won the Women's Amateur Championship six times, a record for USGA competitions. Between 1928 and 1931, Collett won no less than nineteen consecutive matches - a feat which is as yet unbeaten.

International golf for women began in 1905 when a team from America came to play in the British Ladies' Amateur, but the first ever international women's trophy was the Curtis Cup. The trophy was donated by Harriot and Margaret Curtis, two sisters who had played in the original international event in

1905. America won the first Curtis Cup match in 1932 and dominated the event in subsequent years with a few notable British exceptions including a dramatic win at Prairie Dunes in 1986 which ended a run of thirteen successive American victories.

Women's golf remained largely amateur until 1949 when the Ladies' Professional Golf Association was created in the USA by Patty Berg and Babe Zaharias, two of the major players of the period.

Patty Berg was an enormously talented player and her career records successes in all the major events of the day. She was also a superb ambassador for the women's games as her bubbly personality and good looks drew attention to the sport. It therefore was only right that it should be Berg who became the first president of the USLPGA.

Babe Zaharias, the other founder member of the LPGA, was an equally remarkable golfer. She took up the sport in 1934 at the age of eighteen and immediately impressed fans of the game with her natural prowess.

An all-round athlete, Zaharias also won three Olympic gold medals in 1932, in the javelin, 80m hurdles and the high jump and was a professional baseball and basketball player.

Between 1946 and 1947, Babe won seventeen competitions including the British Ladies' Amateur making her the first American to win the title.

Berg and Zaharias led the way and were followed by such

Patty Berg and Babe Zaharias

outstanding players as Mickey Wright in the 1950s and later Kathy Whitworth and Nancy Lopez, who in the 1970s became the first woman golfing superstar.

Lopez has had an amazing career to date. Her achievements include winning the New Mexico Amateur in 1969 at the tender age of twelve, while in 1975 she was runner-up in the US Women's Open. Renowned for her unusual swing which has variously been described as "loopy", "shut" and "faulty", Lopez went from strength to strength, winning seventeen of her first fifty tournaments on the professional circuit. In only five years she collected over $1 million in prize money and by 1989 this figure had risen to over $3 million.

No doubt the increase in the size of the purse for the women's tournaments was largely due to the fact that golf had become big business, with extensive television coverage and major sponsorship deals.

The Americans dominated their home circuit for many years with most of the major trophies going to local players. One notable exception being Catherine Lacoste of France who, in 1967 at the age of 22, became the youngest ever winner of the US Women's Open. However the European players did begin to catch up and a Tour of Britain and Europe has subsequently been established. One of the leading lights is British player Laura Davies who became the first Briton to win the US Women's Open in 1987.

Davies is a wonderful example of a natural player. She has

never had a formal lesson but has managed nevertheless to dominate the women's game in recent years. Her obvious strength lies in the power she is able to apply to her swing, often hitting the ball further than her male counterparts. Though she believes her greatest gift to be the accuracy of her short game. In 1988 she won events on five separate tours - three in Europe, two in the USA and one each in Thailand, Japan and Australia.

Women's golf is flourishing and the future of the game, for both amateur and professional players, looks very promising indeed.

Laura Davies winning 1987 US Open

The Professionals

❦

Professional golfers are among the best known and most popular sporting heroes of the twentieth century, but it wasn't always so. Until about a hundred years ago golf was very much an amateur sport, and the professionals involved in it were there to make clubs and balls, give lessons to the club members and even carry their bags!

In the 1890s three legendary British golfers ushered in the new era of the professional golfer and played competitive golf internationally to earn a living. Harry Vardon, James Braid and J.H. Taylor dominated the game for two decades and became known as the "Great Triumvirate".

Harry Vardon was the leading member of that outstanding trio. He is credited with inventing the "Vardon grip" - the style of grip still used by today's professionals - which involves overlapping the index finger of the left hand with the little finger of the right. It is actually more likely that Vardon merely popularised the grip, as it was used by several players of the period.

Vardon's swing, however, was quite unique. He played with his left arm bent slightly when common practice at the time was for a rigid left arm. He won his first British Open in 1896 and followed this with wins in 1898, 1899, 1903, 1911 and 1914. This record six wins is still unbroken.

James Braid was something of a slow starter when it came to winning Opens however, and was in his thirties by the time he collected the trophy in 1901. He quickly made up for lost time though, and by 1910 had won the British Open a further four times, in 1905, 1906, 1908 and 1910. When on form he was without doubt the best putter and had the longest hit of the three members of the Triumvirate. In his later years Braid became involved with course design and made quite a reputation for himself as a course architect. One of his best pieces of work must surely be the King's Course at Gleneagles.

J. H. Taylor was the first of the three golfers to come to prominence. He won the British Open in 1894 and, following Vardon and Braid's example, went on to win it a total of five times. A formidable opponent at any time, Taylor excelled in high winds because the characteristic low flight of his ball made his game less susceptible to such conditions than his contemporaries. In 1933 he was captain of Great Britain's victorious Ryder Cup Team. Taylor was also instrumental in the foundation of the first Professional Golfers' Association in 1901.

Huge crowds followed the trio wherever they played and, like today's professional golfers, they were asked to endorse

products and make personal appearances that boosted their income.

Of course it wasn't long before the Americans caught up, and in 1911 Johnny McDermott became the first home-grown golfer to win the US Open, though he wasn't the first American golfing hero. That honour was reserved for Francis Ouimet, an amateur golfer from Brookline who, in 1913, took time off work to play in the Open when he heard it was being played at his local course. At the tender age of twenty years he took on the visiting British greats like Harry Vardon and Ted Ray, beating them at their own game to take the title.

It was 1922 before the Americans had their first taste of victory on British soil when Walter Hagen won the Open Championship. For the next decade they were to dominate the tournament through the performances of such golfing heroes as Bobby Jones, Gene Sarazen and Densmore Shute. The British didn't score a home win again until 1934 when Henry Cotton took the title, but by then it was obvious that the United States were the undisputed leaders in the international golf scene.

At this stage the amateur game still produced players that could take on the professionals, and the four major events in the golfing calendar were the US and British Opens and the US and British Amateur Championships - all four were won by Bobby Jones in his grand slam of 1930.

Jones was a superb golfer - his style was flowing and his swing consistent and rhythmical. Despite many lucrative offers he never became a professional, in fact he retired from competitive golf altogether after his grand slam. Never a man who encouraged the attention his talent brought him, Jones played golf for the purest of reasons - his own enjoyment. It was to this end that he and a few friends founded the Augusta National Golf Club. Augusta then became the home of the US Masters Championship after its establishment in 1934, and the emphasis shifted away from the amateur game.

Now all four tournaments known today as "the Majors" were in place - the US and British Opens, the Masters and the USPGA Championship. Amazingly, in 1953, the great American golfer Ben Hogan achieved the feat of winning three of the Majors (the exception being the USPGA), a record which has yet to be beaten.

Ryder Cup

By the 1950s the game had taken on a new status brought about by the financial rewards and the advent of television. There's no doubt Arnold Palmer was a superb golfer, but it was television that made him the first real golfing superstar as he played daily in millions of homes across America. The power of television also began to dictate game play including replacing the matchplay formula in professional tournaments with four rounds of strokeplay on separate days; players were now matched against the course rather than one another.

In the 1960s Arnold Palmer, Jack Nicklaus and Gary Player, a South African, dominated the game, both on and off television. They became household names, even to people who knew nothing about golf, and were golf's first millionaires.

However, by the end of the 1970s the Europeans began to stage something of a comeback. In 1976 a young Spaniard burst on to the international golf scene. The nineteen-year-old Severiano Ballesteros emerged as a remarkable talent in his challenge for the 1976 Royal Birkdale Open. His form was impressive and he captured the attention of the media and public alike with his easy grace and poise.

A few years later, in 1979, Ballesteros won his first British Open and then set about making his name on the American circuit. He did this with some style by winning the US Masters, the first European ever to win the competition and, at 23, the youngest champion in that tournament. Other Europeans followed: Sandy Lyle won the British Open in 1985, while in the same year Germany's Bernhard Langer won the US Masters. This revival of European golf climaxed with them winning the prestigious Ryder Cup that year.

The Ryder Cup is a biennial competition between British and American professional golfers, instituted in 1927. It had become something of a one-sided affair though, with America's success virtually unchecked until the British team was made the European team in 1979. Following their 1985 victory the Europeans went on to win again in 1987 and tie in 1989.

European players began increasingly to win on American soil, and in 1989 and 1990, England's Nick Faldo won the US Masters, with Welshman Ian Woosnam following his example in 1991.

Arnold Palmer

The Future

❦

The impact of television and the superstar status of modern golfers continues to increase the popularity of the game. Golf has come a long way from its simple Scottish origins and golfers are now not only playing for prestige but for vast amounts of money and lucrative sponsorship deals.

In the last twenty years there has been a significant European revival in golf that coincides with the emergence of a number of notable European players on the professional circuit. The industry is particularly booming in Spain and Portugal, where purpose-built resorts cater to the vast numbers of northern European golfers escaping their inclement winters to play in sunnier climes.

But the most significant expansion of the game has been in the Far East, particularly in Japan where today there are an estimated eight million golfers. There are over four thousand golf courses in Japan, but in a country where space is at a premium and demand far outweighs supply, to join a golf club can cost as much as £250,000. Consequently, although many Japanese golfers own a full set of clubs, as few as fifteen percent will ever play on a course. The others must be content with driving ranges like Tokyo's huge Shiba Park. The other alternative has been to look abroad, and a number of the world's most famous courses, including Turnberry in Scotland and Riviera in the United States are now owned by Japanese corporations.

In addition, today's technology means that golf courses can be created almost anywhere, from swamplands to hillsides. Advances in landscape and irrigation techniques mean that perfect greens can be created in the middle of a desert. And the demand for golf is such that not only are such feats possible but they are in common use.

A notable example of such an achievement is to be seen at the aptly-named Desert Highlands in Arizona, USA. The course was designed by professional golfer Jack Nicklaus and has been described as "a series of green footprints in the desert." It is certainly a remarkable, almost surreal course, and took Nicklaus over two years to plan.

Another Nicklaus course, designed in collaboration with Desmond Muirhead, is New St Andrews in Tochigi, Japan. Located just outside Tokyo, the course is almost a showcase of technological advances. Caddies control a computerised electronic system which carries the players' golf bags while the golfers themselves are transported via a monorail. The course is also floodlit to maximise the availability of play.

Technology has also had effects on the way in which golfers assess their performance. Once a golfer had only his own opinion (and usually those of a few golfing friends!) to figure out where his game was weak. Nowadays he can hook up to a computer which will evaluate his swing, his stance and his weight-to-power ratio. The USGA has invested over $2 million since 1991, to develop a computer programme which systematically breaks down the process of a golf swing into a series of images, captured milli-second by milli-second, which are then portrayed on a screen for evaluation.

Likewise, golf balls now undergo tests similar to those developed to test the aerodynamics of cars, and materials such as thermo-plastics and other equally innovative substances, are already important in the production of both golf ball covers and cores.

Golf clubs too are a short step away from being perfected by computer. The invention of the "long putter" which has been met with equal amounts of criticism and adulation is one such example. Others include the use of "square grooves" on the club face of irons to give greater stopping ability to the flight of the ball, and "woods" with metal heads.

Purists, concerned that all the advances in technology will detract from the sportsmanship of the game, need not worry though. Golf's governing bodies and authorities are determined that skill be retained in the game and that any such "improvements" are not capable of ultimately ruining the sport.

Nor are the professional golfers keen on the replacing of technique with gadgets. As Gary Player was once heard to remark on the subject of golf innovations:

"With all the stuff that's coming out, guaranteed someday, on an uphill hole, a player will say: "I don't hit the ball that long, switch on that fan behind me.""

He, like the countless number of weekend players who head to their local course for a round or two, knows that golf's real strength lies not in perfection, but in the pleasure it brings to millions around the globe.